Quilts in My Cubicle

Barbara Holtzman

Located in Paducah, Kentucky, the American Quilter's Society (AQS) is dedicated to promoting the accomplishments of today's quilters. Through its publications and events, AQS strives to honor today's quiltmakers and their work and to inspire future creativity and innovation in quiltmaking.

Text © 2008, Author, Barbara Holtzman
Artwork © 2008, American Quilter's Society

Executive Editor: Andi Milam Reynolds
Editor: Cassia Farkas Ward
Graphic Design: Barry Buchanan
Cover Design: Michael Buckingham
Photography: Charles R. Lynch

Additional copies of this book may be ordered from the American Quilter's Society, PO Box 3290, Paducah, KY 42002-3290, or online at www.AmericanQuilter.com.

Library of Congress Cataloging-in-Publication Data

Holtzman, Barbara.
    Quilts in my cubicle/by Barbara Holtzman.
        p. cm.
    ISBN 978-1-57432-963-6
    1. Patchwork--Patterns. 2. Quilting--Patterns. I. Title.
    TT835.H556236 2008
    746.46'041--dc22

                                    2008038863

American Quilter's Society
P. O. Box 3290 • Paducah, KY 42002-3290
www.AmericanQuilter.com

Proudly printed and bound in the United States of America

Dedication

To my husband, Tom, who doesn't always "get" my quilting, but accepts and brags on it anyway!

Acknowledgments

To Bonnie Sherman, who gave me her last scrap of a fabric that she was using, but it was what I needed to finish my quilt. She also checked my copy for corrections and made suggestions. She was constantly encouraging and affirmed what I was doing! Thanks, Bonnie!

To Mary Lee for being a friend who just happens to love to quilt.

To Donna Knight for letting me bounce ideas off her and push the envelope just a little further.

As I wrote this book, I was thinking of all the "cubicle" people. I spend eight hours a day in mine, and it always pleases me to look up and see something I created. The compliments from coworkers aren't bad either!

About This Book

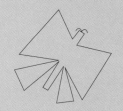

I think there are many working women who sew and need a creative outlet. They are looking for a project that is fun and challenging to do, but that can be completed in a limited amount of free time. They need color and interest to improve their personal space in the cubicles or offices where they spend working time. Having something that they have made themselves makes it that much better!

This book provides fairly simple but eye-catching small quilts that can be made in 6 to 12 hours. If a quilter can sew for a half hour or so three or four nights a week, a small quilt can be done in about a month.

In my cubicle I have a wooden heart, and in the center is a hook for a small wooden plaque that depicts a symbol for the month – a heart for February, a flag for July – and so on. I thought it would be much nicer to have a small handmade quilt to display for each month. Look for the **Make It Your Own!** suggestions with each month's quilt for ideas to change the quilts to fit your own personal style.

This book was written for workers with limited free time, but it could also be for that stay-at-home mom with small children and a busy schedule, or the retired person who is looking for something cute and fun to make as a gift or charitable donation.

Each project section includes a picture of the quilt, cutting and sewing directions, and a full-size pattern that can be copied or traced. There are tips for that month's quilt that provide extra help for sewing.

This book gives a beginner with minimal experience a chance to make something almost "no fail." A more experienced sewer will also be able to easily follow the directions and customize a project to make something that is all their own. These are not art quilts, but there is enough freedom from conventional quilts to provide a very creative outlet.

Have fun making your own, personal, small cubicle quilt!

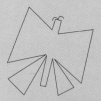

Contents

PROJECTS

Glossary

▼ FUSSY CUT

Selectively place the pattern piece on fabric and choose what you want to show on the quilt.

I used this technique in the BUTTERFLIES ARE FREE TO FLY May block for the butterfly wings and body.

▼ GRADE THE SEAM

This is the process of trimming the seam allowance. If one piece is light and the other dark and the seam will be pressed to the light, trim the dark seam about ⅛" to avoid its shadowing through the front.

▼ IN THE DITCH

In quilting, seams are usually pressed to one side. From the top, sew along the edge of the seam that the fabric has not been pressed to – what I call the "downstream" side. It makes the stitching practically invisible.

▼ PIN BASTE

Prior to quilting, no matter what size the quilt, I use safety pins (about 1") to secure the front, back, and batting. I remove them as I quilt.

▼ REPEATS

In a yard of fabric there is always some kind of repeat (except batiks). They may be small, say ¾" or larger, 3-4" or more. In the WIND FARM March quilt, the stripe I wanted to use was only repeated three times across the width of the fabric. Because of that I had to buy more fabric to be sure I had enough of the stripes to fussy cut all the pieces I needed. Completely cool.

▼ ROUGH CUTS

These are pieces cut the general size of the pattern piece, plus a generous allowance for seams. If the finished piece is 2" square, I might rough cut a 2½" x 2½" square of fabric. I usually use rough cuts when I need several pieces the same size and don't need to cut exact sizes. This also lets you cut your piece along the grain line.

▼ TEARAWAY WEBBING OR STABILIZER

Place this under the block to do some special stitching such as a satin stitch around a petal or sun. After stitching it can be gently torn away. With this product there will not be the waviness or stretching of the fabric that sometimes happens without a stabilizer.

Paper Piecing

The directions here use the small heart block from February as a model (page 20, CRAZY LOVE).

Photocopy or trace the pattern and cut it out. Following the number sequence on the pattern, lay the wrong side of the first piece of fabric against the wrong side of the pattern, covering the #1 section, making sure to overlap all the edges by at least ¼". Pin the fabric piece to the pattern. See figure 1.

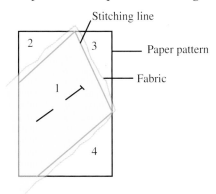

Stitching line

Paper pattern

Fabric

Fig. 1

Rough cut a second piece of fabric to the size of the #2 pattern section, allowing about ½" on all sides. Place the right side of this piece against the right side of the first fabric piece, lining up sewing edges. With the pattern facing you, hold the work up to the light to make sure the stitching line is covered.

Using a smaller stitch, about 1.75, sew right through the paper along the line between section #1 and section #2, starting ¼" before the seam line, and ending ¼" after the seam line. (If it's a seam that will be crossed by another seam later, you only need to overlap by 2–3 stitches, before and after.)

Fold back the pattern and trim the seam. Press from the front (right side of fabric), pressing fabric piece #2 over pattern section #2.

Continue adding pieces in this way, being sure to follow the number sequence on the pattern.

Freezer-paper Piecing

Freezer-paper piecing is similar to paper piecing, but you never sew through the paper—only alongside a fold. I like it because it is accurate and has the added bonus of not having to tear little bits of paper out when you're done.

Almost any paper-pieced pattern can be made out of freezer paper. The only ones that might be more difficult are the smaller, more intricate blocks, such as the 2" Flower blocks in the April quilt INTO EVERY LIFE SOME RAIN MUST FALL; those are probably better with paper piecing.

Patterns are drawn on the dull side of the freezer paper, which creates a reverse of your pattern. **Patterns in this book are already reversed for you.** Lay your freezer paper on top of the pattern and trace, using a fine-line maker. Copy the numbers and colors onto your freezer paper, then finger-fold the pattern along all lines.

One advantage of freezer-paper piecing is that you can see before you sew if the fabic piece you cut is going to cover the whole pattern area. Measurements for fabric are sometimes given for "rough cuts." These are just generous-sized pieces that are the approximate shape of your pattern piece. This method is also a good way to make sure your fabric is on the grain line—just line up a piece and sew! **For patterns that are only used once, you will cut the fabric piece as you go.**

Another advantage is that if you want to press your seam in a different direction, you just lift the freezer paper, press the seam, and then press the freezer paper back down. This technique is used in the windows of the schoolhouse in September's SCHOOL DAZE and in the tree trunks in October's PUMPKIN PATCH.

Freezer-paper Piecing

The patterns in this book are only used once or twice, so I make an original freezer-paper pattern for each block. **If you want to duplicate the block many times,** copy the pattern on regular paper, then staple 5-6 sheets of freezer paper below it, shiny side up, and machine stitch along the pattern lines without thread in the needle.

Patterns do not allow for a ¼" seam allowance, so when you trim the finished block, be sure to add this.

HOW-TO

The directions here use December's STARRY NIGHT pattern on page 58 as a model. It's a good one for learning freezer-paper piecing as it's fairly easy to see how this technique works.

Press section #1 of the shiny side of the freezer paper pattern to the wrong side of your rough-cut fabric—gold, in this instance. See figure 2. Fold back the freezer paper along the line between sections 1 and 2.

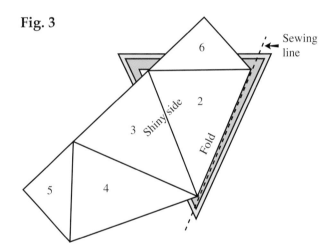

Fig. 3

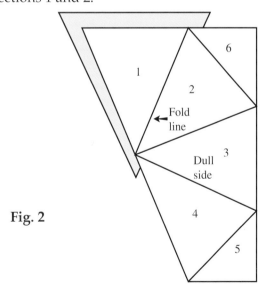

Fig. 2

With the freezer-paper piece facing you, place this unit onto your next fabric piece (red), right sides together. Check to make sure the red piece is big enough to cover its section (#2), then sew right along the edge of the fold. See figure 3.

Trim the edge to about ¼" and grade the seam. Flip the freezer pattern piece open, and press along the seam line on the fabric side, pressing the piece towards the shiny side of the freezer paper.

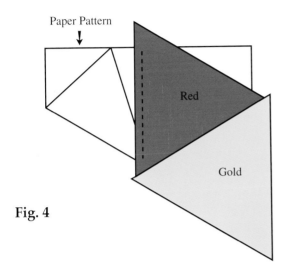

Paper Pattern

Red

Gold

Fig. 4

Turn the work over and press again from the the dull side of the freezer paper, "sticking" the freezer paper to the fabric. Fold back the next line between pattern sections #2 and #3, and continue on until all pieces (#3, #4, #5, and #6) are sewn.

Trim the center edges of the half-blocks only, leaving ¼" seam allowance. Pair off the half-blocks. See figure 5.

To make your center seam accurate, lengthen your stitch to about 2.5. Place a pin vertically where the centers meet. Then place a pin through both pattern pieces about an inch on either side of this vertical pin. Remove the vertical pin. Baste through the center between the pins. Check your seam and make sure the centers meet correctly. If so, restitch the whole seam at 1.75. If not, pull the basting thread out, realign, and try again. It may take a little time to get it right, but your block will look much better because you took the the time to align it correctly.

Fig. 5

Leave the freezer paper in while sewing the blocks together. Trim the block to 4½" square. When you've pieced it with the other blocks, it's a snap to just pull off your freezer paper!

If you have a hard time sewing that perfect ¼" seam—cut border strips 1" wide (or wider!) and trim to the correct width after they are sewn on.

Mitered Corners

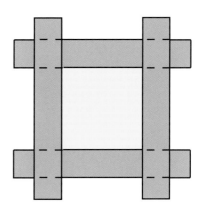

Fig. 7

Mitered corners add a professional-looking final touch to the borders of quilts. You can make any of the borders in this book mitered if you prefer.

When cutting the border strip, figure its length as the size of the inside block plus twice the width of the border, plus another two inches. Center a border strip on top of your block. Stitch along the seam line, stopping and starting ¼" before the beginning and end of the block backstitching to lock the stitch. See figure 6. Sew a strip in the same way along the bottom of the block.

Using a 12½" square ruler, fold and pin the strips at each corner until they form an exact 45-degree angle. See figure 8. Firmly press each corner.

Sew with ¼" seam.
Stop ¼" from edge,
then backstitch.

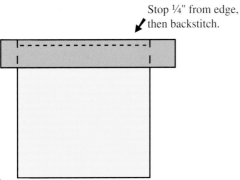

Fig. 6

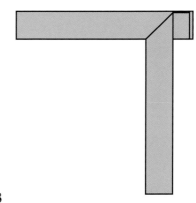

Fig. 8

In the same manner, sew border strips to the sides of the block. Press all borders to the outside. You'll see that the side strips automatically lie over the top and bottom strips. See figure 7.

Carefully pin the corner from the underside, opening up the pressed edge. Draw a light line with a pencil along the pressed fold. Sew along this line from the outside edge to the inside, up to the seam stitching you did previously, then backstitch. **Be careful not to get any of the rest of the top in your stitching—you should only be stitching the remainder of your seam.** Check with your ruler that you still have a true 45-degree seam. If it's good, press open the seam and trim the loose fabric ends. Sew the other three corners the same way.

When the quilt has been layered and quilted, baste just inside the ¼" sewing line all around the quilt. Trim off excess batting and backing.

I use a single-fold binding for my small quilts, cut 1¼" in width. To create a long length of pieced binding, cut several strips of binding fabric. Cut each strip end, top and bottom, at a 60-degree angle. Place two pieces right sides together, overlapping so that ¼" hangs out. See figure 9. Sew a ¼" seam. Press open and cut off the dog-ears.

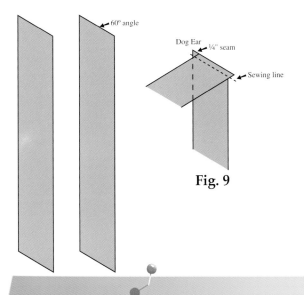

Fig. 9

I accidentally cut some strips at 60 degrees and found they pieced easier than 45-degree cuts. The trick is to cut the top and bottom of the strip at the same angle, and you'll never have to worry about piecing correctly, they just "fit!" However, because you cut your angles before sewing, it's extra important to starch well so there is no stretching.

Lay about 8" of binding along the side of the quilt, right sides together. Start sewing about 3" from the corner, leaving 5" loose to join later. Stop sewing ¼" from the corner and backstitch. Fold the strip up, then down, as shown in figure 10. Sew this side starting at the corner and ending ¼" from the next corner. Repeat for each side.

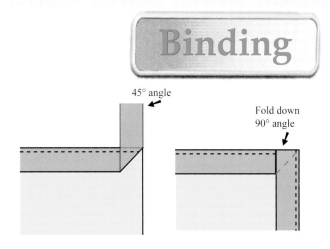

Fig. 10

When you get past the last corner, sew about 3". Lay the first loose end of binding on top of this loose end and draw a line along the 60-degree cut. Add ½" to this mark and draw a pencil line, which will be your cutting line. Cut off the excess. Now your strips should lie with one strip ½" longer than the other. See figure 11.

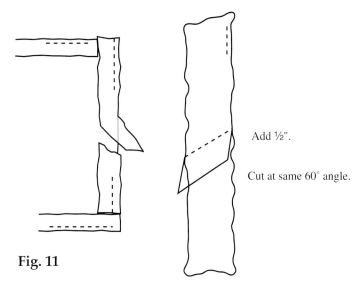

Add ½".

Cut at same 60° angle.

Fig. 11

Align the 60-degree cuts so you will have a ¼" seam with the overlaps, as in figure 9. Sew the seam and carefully press open. Trim the dog ears. Finish sewing the binding along the edge of the quilt. Press the binding to the outside along the seam to get a nice crisp edge. Roll the binding to the back of the quilt and blindstitch it down, making sure it is an even width all along the front of the quilt.

Time

Since I work full time and have a husband whom I want to see now and then, I have to get creative about my time for sewing. I'm always **thinking ahead** in my mind about the next step on a quilt: is it a seam, basting for quilting, cutting strips, or unsewing? If I know what my next step is, I wait for a few open minutes, and when they come along, I'm ready!

I do a lot of my handwork during my 15-minute morning and afternoon breaks at work. It's amazing what you can get done in those times if you're prepared! **It's all about fitting in sewing time wherever possible to complete your quilt.** Plan and prepare for those times, and you'll be surprised how quickly a quilt will come together.

Supplies

As far as **fabric** goes, if you have a healthy stash you may not need to purchase very much. However, I hesitate to recommend this practice, as it can lead to Fabric Withdrawal Syndrome (FWS), a little-known illness among quilters. (I suppose it's little-known because most quilters are constantly buying fabric!)

First, get your **sewing area** set up so that you can sit down if you even have three minutes—a lot can be done in 15 three (3) minute increments!

These aren't big quilts, so you don't need a large area. A chair and small table to hold your machine and supplies handy are all you need. I keep a **TV tray** to the right of my machine with a towel on it for an ironing surface, and the **iron** beside it and ready to plug in. Sometimes when I plug my curling iron in, I plug in my iron, too, and I'm ready to go if I get an extra few minutes in the morning. If you can't plug in an iron close by, get a **wooden iron**—they really do work, especially for paper piecing. [Hint: Half of a wooden clothespin will also work.]

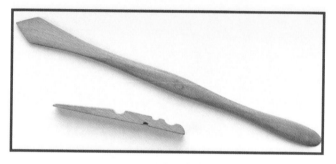

Wood iron and half clothespin

I love my TV trays! You need the nice, wooden, flat-topped ones. In addition to the one beside my machine, I use one in front of the TV—but not to eat! I plug my iron into an **extension cord** (best if you use one with a **circuit-breaker**) and can trim and iron those small pieces while I watch TV. Think of it as a triple return on your time: time spent with your husband (or whoever is in charge of the remote), TV time, and productive sewing time.

One thing I don't recommend doing on a TV tray is cutting pieces with a rotary cutter. I'm speaking from experience when I say that's a big No-No!

I've found that almost any iron will work, as long as it's not one of those that turn off after half an hour. Those are for sissies. If you luck into a good block of time to work, you don't want to have the iron cold when you reach for it! Almost all the ironing I do is with a **dry iron**. The only time I use **steam** is for blocking a quilt.

Starch is important because it stabilizes the fabric and gives it some body. You can buy starch in cans, dry or liquid. I personally like the liquid since it's quick and easy to mix in my own **spray bottle**. Starch your fabric to the consistency of lightweight paper. However, since starch is a corn product, bugs like it. After your quilt is finished, be sure to soak it gently in cool water to remove the starch, then lay it face up on a **couple of towels** to dry.

Techniques

The blocks in this book are almost all based on 2" increments, from 4", 8", to 10", and they can be easily added to, or deleted from, to create the size block or quilt you want. Mix and match to create your own individual small quilt, or enlarge it to whatever size desired. If small blocks scare you, **the 2" blocks can easily be resized** using graph paper or the copy machine, but remember—small quilts are quick to complete!

This book shows you how to make small quilts using a variety of techniques. You'll be **paper piecing** and **freezer-paper piecing**. There will be **template-free sewing**, which is just sewing two blocks together that have been cut to size, such as the 2" block and four 1" blocks sewn in the corners for January SNOWBALL FIGHT. You'll get to use **fusible webbing** and **tearaway interfacing**. Approach each technique with the attitude that you're going to do your best and that's what it will be—your best!

Stitching

I recommend a **stitch length of 1.75** because it's small enough to pierce the paper and make it easier to tear away, but large enough to fit your seam ripper. Sometimes with these smaller pieces, though, it's easier just to start a block over than to rip it out (trust me on this one!).

With small blocks, I'll cut and sew several extra so I can pick and choose the most "correct" size. I'll use the extra for my label. A **size 8 needle** makes a smaller hole, and when you use it along with **50- or 60-weight thread**, you'll see a difference in the size of the block. A larger needle and thicker thread take up more room so your block may be slightly smaller.

I use **light gray thread** for almost all my basic sewing, but will switch to a color matching the fabric when the thread may show through to the front.

Use your **walking foot** whenever possible. Even with small pieces, it's easy to have fabric move and the walking foot prevents slippage. It's especially nice to use the walking foot when quilting in the ditch—it helps keep everything even. My walking foot has a **mark for the ¼" seam**, so it helps with accuracy.

The **single-hole throat plate** is also a big plus, especially for small blocks. I've read much by people who really recommend them, and I would agree—you'll see the difference when you use one. Your small pieces won't get "eaten" by the machine.

After you have sewn two seams together, check with your **ruler** to make sure your ¼" seam is true, and each piece is accurate. You'll have less frustration later on if you check at each step and make adjustments as needed. My favorite is the 12½" square ruler. As I put together blocks, I can easily check them to see if they are square. Make any corrections (unsewing or remaking) as needed. You'll be rewarded with a correctly sized block and quilt if you do this all along the way.

General Directions

Borders

Quilt borders are like the matting for a picture; they help to frame and set off your work of art. Each pattern in this book has allowances and gives measurements for at least one border.

Because borders are a great way to highlight your design, you are encouraged to personalize your quilt by choosing colors or fabrics other than those suggested. Whether you want to spark up your quilt with a favorite bright color, or try a certain combination of strips to complement your decor, it's fun to play around with effects by laying different border possibilities along your finished block before you make a final choice.

To figure the amount of fabric you will need to cut, first measure your block from top to bottom through the very center of your quilt and cut 2 strips to that measurement. On my inside borders, I often call for ¾" strips, but you can determine what width you want. Sew these strips to the sides of your block and press the strips to the outside edges.

Now measure from left to right across the center of the block with the 2 side borders in place. Cut 2 strips to that measurement. Sew these to the top and bottom of the block. Press toward the outside edge.

Repeat this measuring process to add the next border, if indicated or desired.

Finishing

When you finish with the top, **block it** before you layer and quilt. This is done by pinning it, right side down, to a grid with 1" increments. Sometimes I pin it to my TV tray with the towel on it, and use my 12½" square ruler to check for straight lines and correct border lines.

Next, spray the top (lightly) with starch, and iron with a hot, dry iron to set the seams. **Iron the back first and then the front.** This will really make it easier to machine quilt and flattens it out nicely.

Layer the quilt with batting and backing, then **pin-baste** every 3" to 4".

I like to use a walking foot and sew all the borders and seams first. This locks everything down for the free-motion quilting. I use matching thread and sew on the **"downstream" side** – the side of the seam that does **not** have the seam allowance pressed on it. Starching your backing fabric also helps with quilting the layers together. If I have pinned well and starched well, I don't worry about shifting because the block is so small.

In each pattern, an allowance is made for cutting **binding** out of a certain fabric, which usually matches the border. Don't be afraid to change to a different color for a great contrast. This is another way to be creative and personalize your quilt.

Add another fat quarter in the color you want for your **backing**. Some people like to match the front, others want to use up extra material. Just make it appropriate to what you're sewing, so that the back is as nice as the front.

For an easy **rod pocket or sleeve**, cut a 5" strip as long as the width of the quilt. Iron under ¼" twice on each 5" end and sew along that edge. Fold the strip in half lengthwise and baste raw edges along the top edge of the quilt, making sure to keep the binding already attached to the quilt front out of the way. When you sew down the binding to the quilt by hand around the quilt, you'll cover the rod pocket back raw edge. Catch-stitch, whipstitch, or blindstitch along the sides and bottom of the rod pocket, allowing about ⅛" ease for the diameter of the rod so the front of the quilt stays flat.

SNOWBALL FIGHT

13" x 13", by the author.
Snowballs are stacked up, waiting for the first throw!

January

Quilt Size: 13" square
Block Size: 1½" square

Fabric

White: Fat eighth
Blue: Fat quarter
Purple: At least 4" x 11"

Prewash, starch, and press fabric before cutting.

Cutting

White: 21 squares, 2" x 2" (snowballs)

Blue: 84 squares, 1" x 1" (snowball corners)
    4 strips, 2" x 14" (outside border)
    2 (A) strips, 2" x 3½"
    2 (B) strips, 2" x 5"
    1 (C) strip, 2" x 2"
    1 (D) strip, 2" x 6½"
    Strip(s) to equal 1¼" x 70" (binding)

Purple: 4 strips, ¾" x 11" (inside border)

    15" square for backing
    15" square of white batting

Construction

On the back of each 1" blue square, draw a pencil line diagonally across from corner to corner. Place a blue square on the corner of each white square as shown in figure 1. Sew along the diagonal line, adding another blue square to each white corner as you sew around the block.

Trim the blue squares outside of the stitching line and press to the corner (figs. 2 and 3). Don't trim the 2" white square. Use the white base square to align your seams when sewing. While the blue block may shift a little, the white block will give you the correct sewing edge.

This is a "get out your TV tray, sit in front of the TV, trim, and press" time. Don't forget to iron on a towel!

Line up the squares and rectangles according to the quilt assembly. Sew vertical rows. See the Tip on page 17.

Join the rows together. Press seams open as you sew. You may have to grade the seams to make sure the blue doesn't show through on the white. The quilt top should measure 9½" x 9½" at this point.

Fig. 1

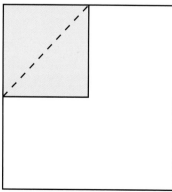

Fig. 2

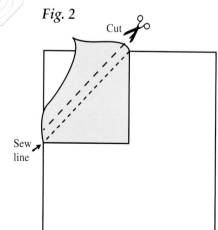

Cut

Sew line

Fig. 3

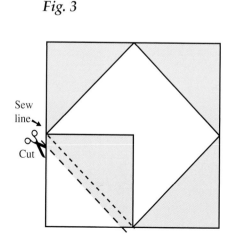

Sew line

Cut

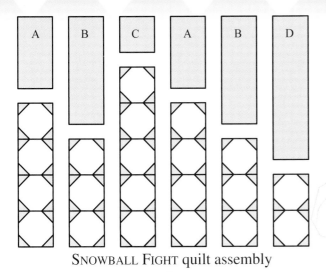

SNOWBALL FIGHT quilt assembly

Set your stitch length to a longer stitch, about 2.5, and stitch the Snowball blocks together one at a time. Check the seam on the right side to make sure the corners on the snowball meet correctly. If they do, great— resew with your stitch length at 1.75. If they don't match, pull the bobbin thread to release the stitching, reset the blocks, and sew again. It takes a little longer initially to do this, but then you're assured of having beautifully matching seams, which can be hard to do on smaller blocks.

Make It Your Own!

▼ Forget the sky and make the whole quilt out of Snowball blocks using novelty scraps that are fussy cut for subject matter – kind of an "I Spy" quilt.

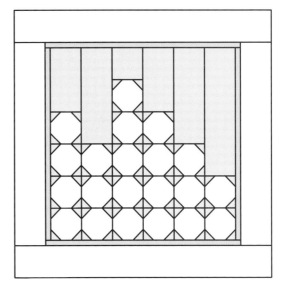

▼ Hot-fix crystals, iridescent beads, or metallic thread would look great on this quilt.

▼ Make one Snowball block pale yellow for that "Don't eat yellow snow!" look.

Borders

See page 14 for instructions on borders.

Inside border: Use the purple 11" strips, cut to fit. They should measure 9½" each side, and 10" top and bottom.

Outside border: Use the blue 14" strips, cut to fit. They should measure 10" each side, and 13" top and bottom.

Finishing and Binding

See page 14 for tips on finishing. Square up the quilt. Layer the top over white batting and your backing. Pin baste. Quilt as desired.

See page 11 for instructions on how to make and attach binding.

Crazy Love

12½" x 12½", by the author.

Yes, love is crazy!

Quilt size: 12½" square
Block size: 8" square

Fabric

Red: Fat eighth, plus assorted scraps, some at least 8" long
Orange: At least 4" x 10"
Yellow: Fat eighth

I fussy cut the fabric in the sampler quilt's #1 sections to get a secondary "heart" from the swirls.

Prewash, starch, and press fabric before cutting.

Cutting

Orange:
4 strips, ¾" x 10" (first inside border)

Yellow:
4 strips, ¾" x 10" (second inside border)
Rough-cut pieces for background of heart

Red (from fat eighth):
4 strips, 2" x 13" (outside border)
Strips to equal 1¼" x 54" (binding)

14" square for backing
14" square of batting

Construction

See page 7 for instructions on paper piecing.

Copy the pattern on page 21 and cut it in half. Referring to the quilt photo, start with the light red center of the heart, and use red strips to paper piece each side of the heart, following the numbers in sequence. Use a variety of reds.

When each side is pieced, trim the center seam only, leaving ¼" seam allowance. Sew the 2 sides together at the center, pressing the seam open.

Trim the outside edges, leaving ¼" seam allowance. The block should measure 8½" square. Keep the paper in until the borders are sewn on.

Borders

See page 14 for instructions on borders.

First inside border: Use the orange 10" strips, cut to fit. They should measure 8½" each side, and 9" top and bottom.

Second inside border: Use the yellow 10" strips, cut to fit. They should measure 9" each side, and 9½" top and bottom.

Outside border: Use the red 13" strips, cut to fit.

Finishing and Binding

See page 14 for tips on finishing. Square up the quilt. Layer the top over the batting and backing. Pin baste. Quilt as desired.

See page 11 for instructions on how to make and attach binding.

Make It Your Own!

▼ Who says hearts need to be red? How about blue or orange or pink? Or black and white and one other color?

▼ Instead of crazy-piecing the heart shape, trace the outline of the heart and do strictly strip piecing of each side. See figure 1.

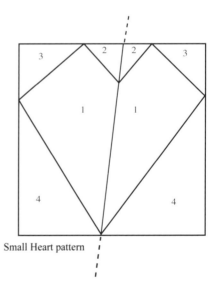

Small Heart pattern

Fig. 2

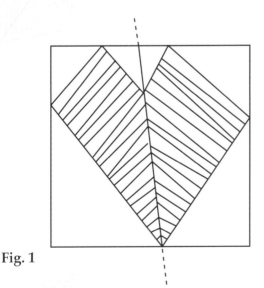

Fig. 1

▼ Make 9 Heart blocks, combine them with sashing and border, and it becomes a larger wallhanging!

▼ See figure 2 for a smaller, paper-pieced 2⅜" square Heart block that can, if you want, be interchanged with some of the other quilt blocks in this book.

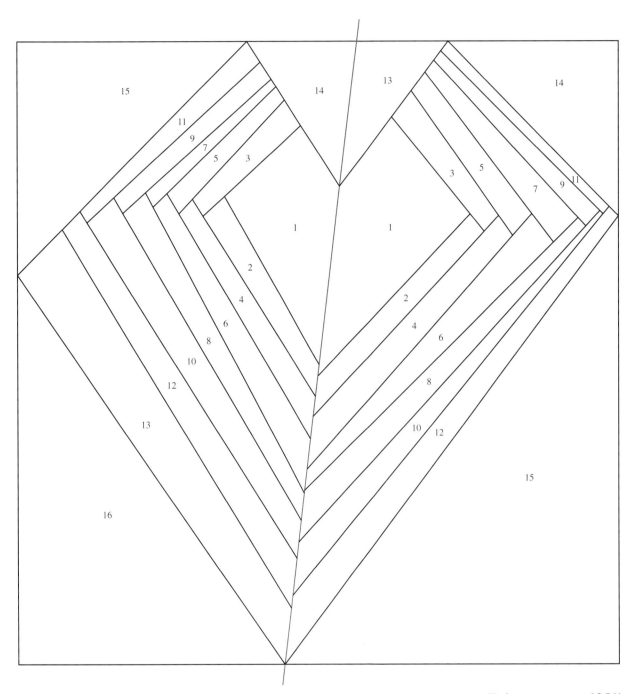

CRAZY LOVE pattern   *Enlarge pattern 125%*

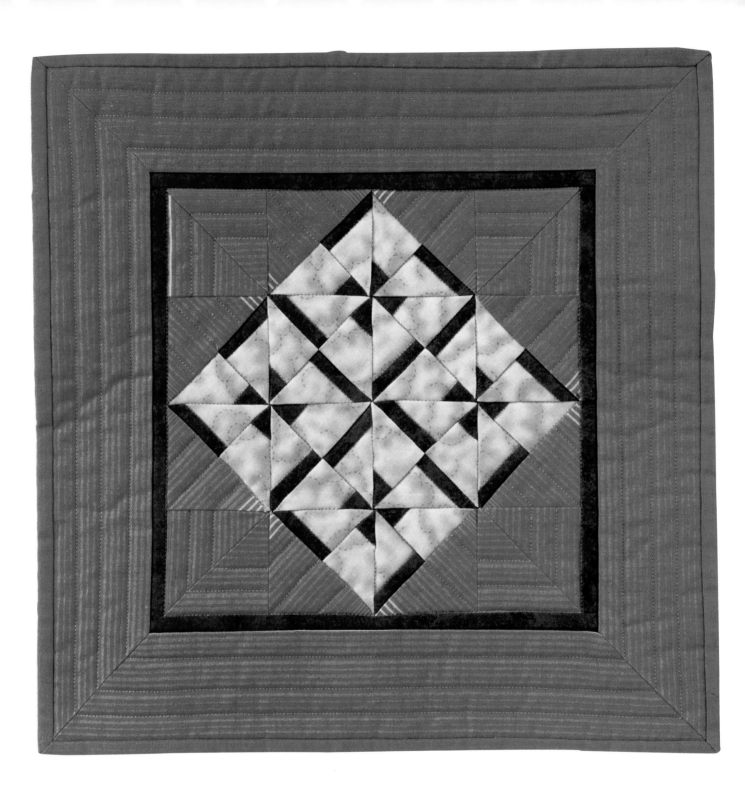

WIND FARM

13" x 13", by the author.

Out on the open plains, it seems like the wind is always blowing!

Quilt size: 13" square
Block size: 2" square

Fabric:

Purple: Fat quarter
Blue sky: Fat quarter
Stripe: Fat quarter

> To get the look I had in mind, I used a sky-printed fabric, and I bought 1½ yards of a varied stripe. The particular stripe I wanted only had two repeats, so I used just two 3" widths out of the fabric. The rest will get used another day in another quilt!

Prewash, starch, and press fabric before cutting.

Cutting

Purple:
4 strips, ¾" x 10" (inside border)
Rough-cut strips, to equal 1" x 60" (freezer-paper piecing)

Blue:
Rough-cut strips, to equal 3" x 60" (freezer-paper piecing)

Stripe:
4 strips, 2½" x 15" (outside mitered border)
Strips to equal 1¼" x 60" (binding)
4 squares, 3" x 3", cut on grain, stripes vertical
4 squares, 3" x 3", cut on bias, with stripes running point to point

15" square for backing
15" square of batting

Construction

> Striped squares are cut slightly larger than needed. After they have been cut into triangles and sewn to make the various blocks, trim to correct 2½".

See figure 1. Cut 2 of the striped, on-grain squares diagonally from top left to bottom right; cut the other 2 diagonally from top right to bottom left.

Sew the A triangles together across long edges. Press. Sew the B triangles together across long edges. Press. The stripes of these blocks will now form chevron patterns.

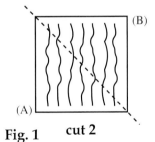 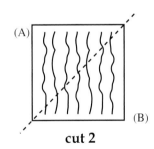

Fig. 1   cut 2   cut 2

Cut all striped, bias squares, as shown in figure 2, page 24. The outside edges of the C triangles will be on bias, so starch well and handle carefully.

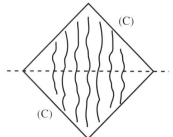

(C)

(C)

Fig. 2

See page 7 for instructions on freezer-paper piecing. Trace the windmill pattern in figure 3 onto the dull side of the freezer paper. You will need 16 of these patterns. Cut each pattern in half as indicated by the dotted line, forming D and E triangles.

Lay the pattern pieces on the wrong side of rough-cut blue strips as shown in figure 4. Press to stick patterns to fabric. Cut fabric apart as indicated by the dotted lines, leaving a generous ¼" around all edges. Fold back freezer paper along the seam lines—at the points of D triangles and along the base of E triangles—and trim seam allowances to ¼".

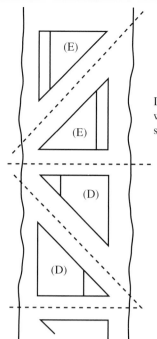

(E)

(E)

(D)

(D)

(D)

Iron freezer-paper triangles to wrong side of blue fabric, shiny side down.

Fig. 4

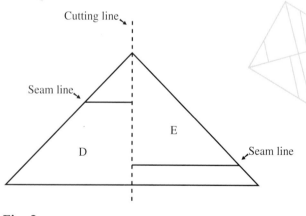

Cutting line

Seam line

E

D

Seam line

Fig. 3

Windmill Pattern
Copy 16 times.

Lay the seam allowances along the rough-cut purple strip and sew, one after another, chain-style along the folded lines of the freezer paper. See figure 5. Cut the pieces apart and grade seam allowances. Unfold patterns and press the purple fabric back over the freezer paper. Trim the purple seam allowance to ¼" around the pattern.

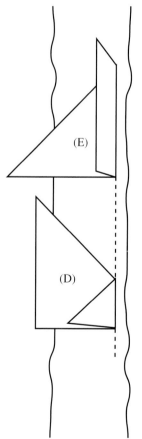

(E)

(D)

Sew (D) and (E) triangles to purple strip, chain style.

Fig. 5

Sew the purple-pointed D triangles to the purple-based E triangles in the configuration shown in the WIND FARM quilt photo on page 22 and the quilt assembly on page 25. Sew 8 of these pieced triangles to the 8 striped C triangles, joining long edges. Sew the remaining pieced triangles into 4 blocks by joining purple-based edges. See figure 6.

Fig. 6

Lay out blocks according to the quilt assembly diagram. Sew into rows. Press all seams in rows in the same direction, alternating the direction for each row. Pin baste the rows together, aligning seams carefully. Sew and press.

Borders

Inside border: Use the purple 10" strips, cut to fit. They should measure 8" each side and 9" top and bottom. See page 14 for instructions on borders. Refer to the quilt photo.

Outside border: Use the 15" strips. See page 10 for instructions on mitered corners.

Finishing and Binding

See page 14 for tips on finishing. Square up the quilt. Layer the top over the batting and backing. Pin baste. Quilt as desired.

See page 11 for instructions on how to make and attach binding.

Make It Your Own!

▼ Fabric choices would change the looks of this quilt. Get a "theme" fabric and fussy cut the triangles.

▼ For a country look, use different plaids and stripes. There are some really cool stripes out there! Find one you like and match your other colors to it.

WIND FARM quilt assembly

INTO EVERY LIFE SOME RAIN MUST FALL

14" x 14", by the author.
When spring flowers start to peep out, it makes the
rainy days much more worthwhile!

Quilt size: 14" x 14"
Block size: 2" square

Fabric

Blue: Scraps of 7–8 different fabrics
Medium green: Fat quarter
Dark green: At least 2" x 11"
Yellow: At least 12" x 18"
Red (or any good flower color): Scraps of different fabrics

Prewash, starch, and press fabric before cutting.

Cutting

Blue:
Rough-cut strips of each fabric, about 2½" x 12" (rain)
4 strips, 1¼" x 10" (inside border)

Medium green:
1 strip, 1" x 9" (grass)
4 strips, 2½" x 15" (outside border)
Strips to equal 1¼" x 64" (binding)

Dark green:
1 strip, 1" x 10½" (leaves)

Yellow:
2 strips, 1" x 9" (strips above flower and above rain)
3 strips, 1" x 2½" (sashing D)
2 strips, ¾" x 2½" (sashing E)
Scraps for background of flowers

16" square for backing
16" square of batting

Construction

See page 7 for instructions on paper piecing. Copy Rain I pattern once and Rain II pattern twice (page 29). Using blue strips, sew them onto a foundation, varying the blue fabrics. Trim each finished Rain strip to 2" wide.

Copy Flower A, B, or C 4 times. Following the directions for paper piecing, sew the Flower blocks, using red, dark green, and yellow fabric.

If using Flower A or B, trim blocks to 2" wide by 2½" long. Add yellow D and E sashing strips between flowers to make a flower strip, as shown in figure 1.

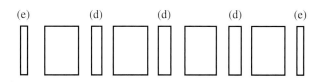

Fig. 1   Sashing strips for use with Pattern A or B

If using Flower C, trim each block to 2½" x 2½" and sew them together without sashing.

Using the quilt photo as a guideline, lay out strips, bottom to top, as follows: medium green strip, flower strip, yellow strip, Rain II strip, Rain I strip, Rain II strip, and another yellow strip at the top. Sew strips together as shown on page 28, trimming and pressing as you go. The quilt should measure 8½" square.

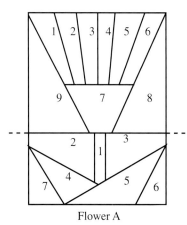

Flower A

April

Borders

See page 14 for instructions on borders. Refer to the quilt assembly diagram.

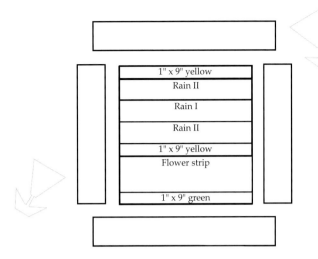

BUTTERFLIES ARE FREE TO FLY quilt assembly

Inside border: Use the blue 10" strips, cut to fit. They should measure 8½" each side and 10" top and bottom.

Outside border: Use the medium green 15" strips, cut to fit.

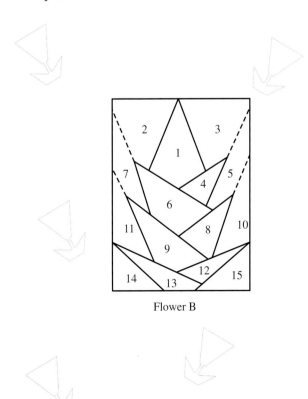

Flower B

Finishing and Binding

Get out your TV tray, tweezers, and the remote, and remove the paper from the blocks.

See page 14 for tips on finishing. Square up the quilt. Layer the top over the batting and backing. Pin baste. Quilt as desired.

See page 11 for instructions on how to make and attach binding.

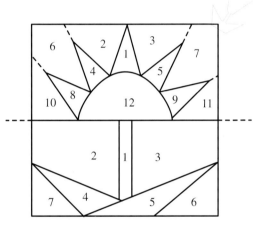

Flower C

Piece #12 on Flower C is zig-zag stitched.

Make It Your Own!

▼ Rain I and Rain II would make an interesting small quilt all on their own. Make 5–9 strips using a variety of dark colors and intersperse them with a bright color every now and then.

▼ Use a variety of colors for the flowers, or even a small colorful print. Three different flower patterns are provided. You can change, mix and match them!

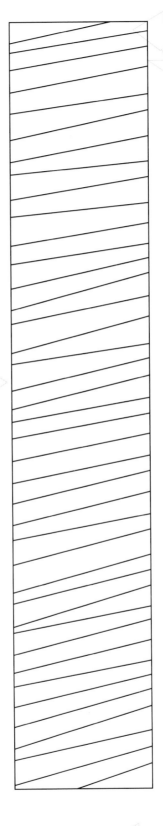

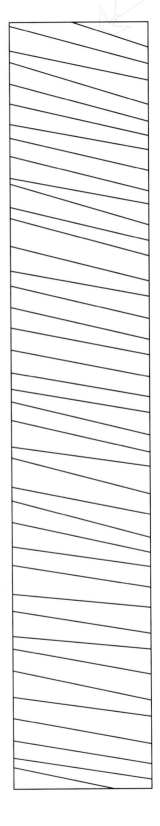

Rain I
Copy once

Rain II
Copy twice

BUTTERFLIES ARE FREE TO FLY

13" x 13", by the author.

Fragile – and magical.

Quilt size: 13" square
Block size: 4" square

Fabric

Dark blue: At least 5" x 12"
Orange print: At least 5" x 10"
Yellow: Fat quarter
Fun border print: Fat quarter
Variety of bright fabrics with fun prints

Prewash, starch, and press fabric before cutting.

Cutting

Dark blue:
4 strips, ¾" x 10" (first inside border)

Orange print:
4 strips, ¾" x 10" (second inside border)

Fun Prints:
Fussy cut as you go for butterfly wings

Fun border print:
4 strips, 2½" x 14" (outside border)
Strips to equal 1¼" x 60"

15" square for backing
15" square of batting

Construction

See page 7 for instructions on freezer-paper piecing.

You can create your own pieced fabric to vary the effects! Sew a 3" x 8" strip of striped or patterned fabric to a 1½" x 8" strip and use it for the wing fabric. The advantage of freezer-paper piecing is you can "see" where to place your fabric before you sew.

Make 2 butterfly patterns (page 32) , tracing each onto the dull side of freezer paper. You will use each freezer-paper pattern twice.

Select prints for butterfly wings. Use the yellow for the background color. Don't forget that with freezer-paper piecing, you can "fussy place" before sewing.

Piece the center/body of the butterfly: sew background fabric to each end of the body fabric; trim outside long edges only.

Place the center/body along one butterfly wing, matching edges with a pin. Sew and trim the seam. Sew the other side, trim, and press both seams towards the center.

Trim the Butterfly blocks to 4½". Sew them to the other Butterfly blocks, using the quilt photo for guidance on placement.

May

Borders

See page 14 for instructions on borders.

First inside border: Use the blue 10" strips, cut to fit. They should measure 8½" each side and 9" top and bottom.

Second inside border: Use the orange 10" strips, cut to fit. They should measure 9" each side and 9½" top and bottom.

Outside border: Use the 14" fun print strips, cut to fit.

Finishing and Binding

Remove freezer paper. Consider these options for butterfly antennae: Outline stitching by hand with one thread of embroidery floss; machine satin stitching; or free-motion stitching, if you're comfortable with that. If you choose machine stitching, be sure to place some tearaway stabilizer underneath.

See page 14 for tips on finishing. Square up the quilt. Layer the top over batting and backing. Pin baste. Quilt as desired.

See page 11 for instructions on how to make and attach binding.

Make It Your Own!

▼ Combine the Butterfly block with Flower blocks from April. The Flower blocks could border the butterflies.

▼ Kids would love this as a larger lap quilt. Add sashing between blocks, or enlarge the pattern for the block 100 percent to 8" to sew even quicker.

▼ Get creative with bead or thread embellishments.

▼ Sew 4 or 5 butterflies across to make a long, narrow quilt or table runner.

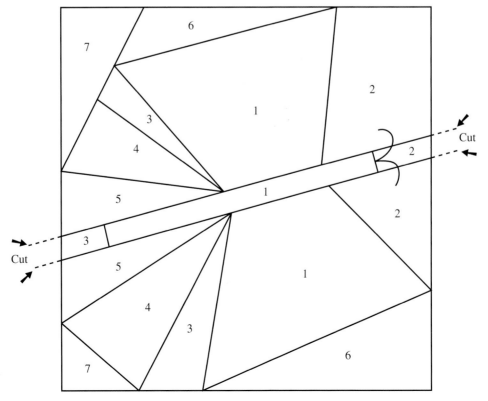

BUTTERFLIES ARE FREE TO FLY freezer-paper assembly

SUNNY DAY

12" × 12", by the author.
For someone not so talented with real flowers,
imaginary ones are wonderful!

Quilt size: 12" square

Fabric

Blue: At least 9" x 9"
Green: Fat quarter, plus scraps of varied greens
Yellow: At least 5" x 5"
Orange: 4 different pieces, one at least 4" x 14"
Tearaway webbing
Fusible webbing

Prewash, starch, and press fabric before cutting.

Cutting

Blue:
1 piece, 7½" x 9"

Green:
4 strips, 2" x 14" (outside border)
Varied strips, 2½" x 10" (piecing for grass)
Strips to equal 1¼" x 58" (binding)

Orange:
4 strips, 1" x 9" (inside border)

14" square for backing
14" square of batting

Construction

See page 7 for instructions on paper piecing. Copy the grass pattern on page 36. Using varied green strips, sew them onto the paper foundation, alternating greens.

Cut a piece of tearaway webbing to 7½" x 9" and trace the sun and flower patterns onto it. Pin the blue sky piece to the tearaway webbing. You'll be able to see the pattern through the sky fabric and won't have to mark your fabric. With free-motion stitching, sew each stem up and down about 4 times, until you have a nice stem.

Following manufacturer's directions for fusible webbing, trace the pattern outlines of the flowers, leaves, and sun onto the paper part of the webbing. Cut out webbing, adding about ¼" to all edges.

Fuse the webbing flower shapes to the wrong side of your different shades of orange fabric, fuse the leaves to the wrong side of the greens, and the sun shapes to the wrong side of the yellow fabric.

Following the outlines of the webbing, cut the shapes from the fabrics, adding a seam allowance to the two sides of the sun that fit in the corner, as shown in the pattern. Fuse the shapes to your sky base, using the pattern as a guide.

With a tight zigzag, almost a satin stitch, sew around the flowers, leaves, sun, and rays. I use 1.25 width and .5 length. Gently pull out the tearaway webbing from behind the block.

Trim the sky and flower piece, allowing ¼" seam allowance along the bottom. Trim the top and bottom of the grass strip. Sew the sky and flower piece to the grass strip. Trim the block to an 8½" square. Refer to the quilt photo.

Borders

See page 14 for instructions on borders.

Inside border: Use the orange 10" strips, cut to fit. They should measure 8½" each side, and 9½" top and bottom.

Outside border: Use the dark green 14" strips, cut to fit.

Finishing and Binding

See page 14 for tips on finishing. Square up the quilt. Layer top over batting and backing. Pin baste. Quilt as desired.

See page 11 for instructions on how to make and attach binding.

Make It Your Own!

▼ Create your own flowers, or use the other "organic" patterns in this book.

▼ Change the scene: remove a flower, or add a butterfly or a tree!

▼ Make a four season wallhanging using these patterns: October (PUMPKIN PATCH) for fall, January (SNOWBALL FIGHT) for winter, May (BUTTERFLIES ARE FREE TO FLY) or April (INTO EVERY LIFE SOME RAIN MUST FALL) for spring, and June (SUNNY DAY) for summer.

Sun pattern plus rays

Flower patterns

Leaf pattern

Stem pattern

Grass pattern

SUNNY DAY patterns

Enlarge pattern 125%

CELEBRATE

12½" x 12½", by the author.

Hope springs eternal!

July

Quilt size: 12½" square

Fabric

Let the fabric do the work for you! Pick a variegated fabric that has "sparks" on it!

Variegated (ranging dark to bright): Fat quarter
Purple: Fat quarter

Prewash, starch, and press fabric before cutting.

Cutting

Variegated:
4 strips, 1" x 10" (inside border)
Rough-cut triangles as needed for fireworks

Purple:
4 strips, 2" x 14" (outside border)
Rough-cut pieces as needed for background
Strips to equal 1¼" x 58" (binding)

14" square for backing
14" square of batting

Construction

See page 7 for instructions on paper piecing. Copy the fireworks patterns on page 39. Cut the pattern apart into strips A–E. Or, if you're feeling more confident about freezer-paper piecing, trace the pattern on the dull side of the freezer paper, and refer to page 7 for instructions on freezer-paper piecing.

Piecing as you go, sew scraps on the strip foundations. Arrange fireworks triangles to go from darker at the bottom to lighter yellows and reds at the top. Use purple for the background color.

Rough cut each triangle of the fireworks before you start sewing and lay them out on your TV tray. You'll have a good idea of what the final piece will look like and you can change out colors as you like, before you sew.

When each strip is pieced, trim only the sides. Lay out your fireworks strips. Before sewing strips together, place a pin to align edges of the paper pattern. This isn't a pattern that needs to match exactly, but line them up as closely as possible. Sew on the lower corner pieces F and G. Trim the block to 8½" x 8½".

Borders

See page 14 for instructions on borders.

Inside border: Use the 10" strips, cut to fit. They should measure 8½" each side and 9½" top and bottom.

Outside border: Use the purple 14" strips, cut to fit.

Finishing and Binding

Carefully pull out the paper pieces. See page 14 for tips on finishing. Square up the quilt. Layer the top over the batting and backing. Pin baste. Quilt as desired.

See page 11 for instructions on how to make and attach binding.

Make It Your Own!

▼ This would be a good quilt with gradations of fabrics in solid colors or prints.

▼ Draw more Flying Geese triangles into the bottom corner pieces and you have a Fan pattern.

▼ Use metallic fabrics for a scintillating, glitzy look.

▼ Embellish with sparkly beads or threads.

Cutting Lines

CELEBRATE pattern

Enlarge pattern 125%

ANT FARM

14" x 14", by the author.

Long ago I had an ant farm for a science project.

I always wondered what Mom would say if they got out!

Quilt size: 14" square
Block Size: 2" square

Fabric

Multi-shaded brown: Fat eighth
Orange: Fat quarter
Yellow: At least 2" x 12"
Green: Scraps of 6–7 different prints, one at least 4" x 12"
Fusible webbing
Black fine point permanent marker

Prewash, starch, and press fabric before cutting.

Cutting

Multi-shaded brown:
27 quarter-squares (see pattern, page 43)
Rough-cuts as needed for blocks

Orange:
4 strips, 2" x 15" (outside border)
Rough-cuts as needed for blocks
Strips to equal 1¼" x 64" (binding)

Green:
4 strips, ¾" x 12" (inside border)
Rough-cuts, 1" x 2" (for grass strip)

Yellow:
1 strip, 1½" x 11"

16" square for backing
16" square of batting

Construction

See page 7 for instructions on paper piecing. Copy the block patterns the number of times noted for each. If you want more possibilities in laying out your ant farm, make several more of each; then you can decide how you want your tunnels to go. This quilt uses paper piecing for the straight seams and fusible webbing for the curved corner pieces.

Fusible quarter-squares for blocks A, C, and D: Trace 27 brown, curved corner pieces on fusible webbing, allowing at least ¾" between pieces. Cut out each quarter-square. Follow manufacturer's directions to fuse webbing to the different blocks, as indicated on patterns.

For these small blocks, it's easier to make the block slightly larger, then trim the block to the exact size after the piecing is done. I suggest making blocks at least 2¾", then cutting them down to 2½" after piecing. Simply add a little extra to the pieces along any outer edge of a block.

For Block A: Following directions for paper piecing, place orange fabric to cover the upper corner of the pattern square, then sew brown strips to each side. Press and fuse a brown, curved corner piece to each Block A. With a zigzag stitch, sew down the curved seam.

For Block B: Following directions for paper piecing, sew brown, then orange, then brown strips to each block pattern.

For Block C: Pin a piece of orange fabric to cover the middle. Then sew a brown strip to one side of the pattern, and cover the other half with orange fabric. Place 2 brown, curved corner pieces with the fusible webbing on top of the orange fabric at each corner. Press. With a zigzag stitch, sew down the curved seams.

For Block D: Pin orange fabric to the pattern, allowing at least ⅜" seam allowance on each side. Press 4 brown, curved corner pieces with fusible webbing to the corners, checking pattern lines before you fuse. With a zigzag stitch, sew down the curved seams.

> You will notice that I didn't match the brown, curved corners exactly. They can vary—because this is an ant tunnel, after all!

Trim each square to 2½". Lay the blocks out according to the quilt photo—or create your own variation! Join the blocks into strips. After sewing each strip, press all seams in the same direction, alternating directions for each strip, so when you join the strips they will fit together much easier.

To add the ants, practice first on a scrap of orange fabric with a fine point permanent marker. Use the quilt photo as a guide.

Copy the pattern on page 43 for the grass. Following the directions for paper piecing, sew grass using varied strips of green fabric. Lay out the yellow sky and grass with the Ant blocks following the quilt photo. Sew the rows together. Trim to a 10½" square.

Borders

See page 14 for instructions on borders.

Inside border: Use the 12" green strips, cut to fit. They should measure 10½" each side and 11" top and bottom.

Outside border: Use the orange 15" strips, cut to fit.

Finishing and Binding

Gently pull out the paper piecing. See page 14 for tips on finishing. Square up the quilt. Layer the top over the batting and backing. Pin baste. Quilt as desired.

See page 11 for instructions on how to make and attach binding.

Make It Your Own!

▼ Use block A, but don't put in the curved corner piece. Enlarge the block 200% and copy it 16 times. Make an "I Spy" quilt, placing the fussy-cut material in the corner.

▼ Use only block D and play with colors for the corner pieces so they form fun circles when joined.

▼ Attach "real" plastic ants as embellishments.

▼ Make the outer border from red-checker fabric to represent a picnic tablecloth.

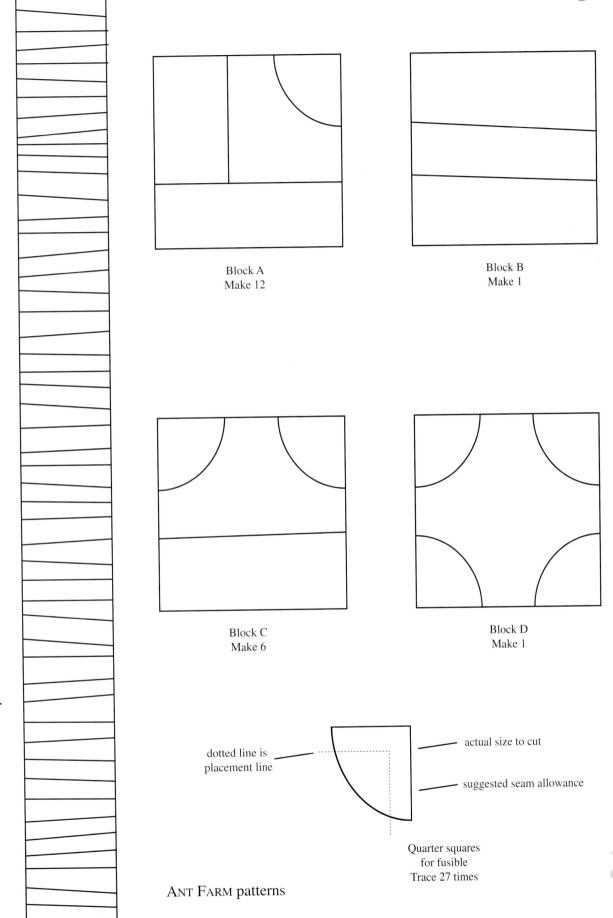

Block A
Make 12

Block B
Make 1

Block C
Make 6

Block D
Make 1

Grass pattern

dotted line is placement line

actual size to cut

suggested seam allowance

Quarter squares
for fusible
Trace 27 times

ANT FARM patterns

SCHOOL DAZE

14" x 14", by the author.
The first day of school holds so much excitement—new clothes—
new books—new friends!

Quilt size: 14" square
Block Size: 2" square

Fabric:

Red: Fat quarter
White: Piece, 11" x 11"
Blue: At least 7" x 13"
Yellow: At least 2" x 10"
Tie-dye: At least 12" x 12"
Scraps of green, grey, black
Fusible interfacing 11" x 11"
Tearaway webbing 11" x 11"
Black fine point permanent marker

Prewash, starch, and press fabric before cutting.

Cutting

Red:
2 rough-cut strips, 1" x 6" (school walls)
Scraps for piecing (around windows)
4 strips, 2" x 15" (outside border)
Strips to equal 1¼" x 64" (binding)

Blue:
4 strips, ¾" × 12" (inside border)
2 rough-cut A strips, 1¼" x 5" (sky beside school)
1 rough-cut B strip, 1¾" x 7" (sky above school)

Yellow:
Rough-cut strip, 2" x 7" (to piece windows)

Green:
2 rough-cut strips, 1¾" x 3¼" (grass)

Grey:
1 rough-cut piece, 2" x 2" (school walk)

Black:
1 rough-cut strip, ¾" x 6½" (school roof)
2 rough-cut pieces, 1½" x 2" (school door)

16" square for backing
16" square of batting

Construction

For Schoolhouse:

See page 7 for instructions on freezer-paper piecing. Copy patterns (page 47) onto the dull side of freezer paper. Piece the schoolhouse walls, windows, and door (2 strips), then the green grass (unit 6) with the gray walk. Trim. Lay out the entire block—units 1, 2 and 3— adding in the roof (unit 7) and sky strips—(unit 8) following the order shown in the block assembly diagram on page 46. Trim the Schoolhouse block to 6½" x 6½".

School kids:

With a pencil, frame out 16 blocks of 2½" on the 11" x 11" white fabric. Allow about ¼" between each block. Trace heads, arms, and legs, following kid patterns on page 47 as guides. Press a layer of fusible interfacing to the wrong side of the fabric.

Sew in the arms, legs, and heads. You can do this by hand, using black or brown embroidery floss and an outline stitch; or by machine, in a small satin stitch or free-motion stitching with tearaway interfacing under the entire piece. Do not cut blocks apart yet!

Trace the outline of clothes on fusible interfacing. Iron them to the back side of the tie-dye material. Cut out the clothes and iron them on to each block. Sew around the clothes with a small zigzag stitch.

September

With a permanent fine point marker, draw in hair, eyes, or any features you like—or leave them plain, as I did. NOW, cut each Kid block to 2½" x 2½". Arrange the blocks in a pleasing pattern.

Assembly:

Lay out the Kid blocks with the Schoolhouse block. Sew together, using the quilt photo as a guide. The block should measure 10½" x 10½".

Borders

See page 14 for instructions on borders and refer to the quilt sample.

Inside border: Use the blue 12" strips, cut to fit. They should measure 10½" on each side and 11" top and bottom.

Outside border: Use red 15" strips, cut to fit.

Finishing and Binding

See page 14 for tips on finishing. Square up the quilt. Layer the top over the batting and backing. Pin baste. Quilt as desired.

See page 11 for instructions on how to make and attach binding.

Make It Your Own!

▼Change out some of the Kid blocks with Flower blocks from April.

▼ Use the 4" Butterfly block from May and surround it with Kid blocks/and or Flower blocks!

▼ Make a quilt with several Schoolhouse blocks in different colors, a Butterfly block from May, and surround with Kid blocks/and or Flower blocks!

▼ Make a quilt with several Schoolhouse blocks in different colors—adding different minor details—and piece together with sashing.

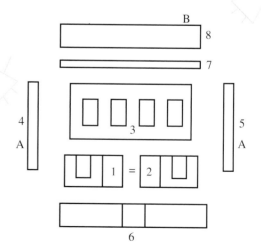

SCHOOL DAZE assembly block

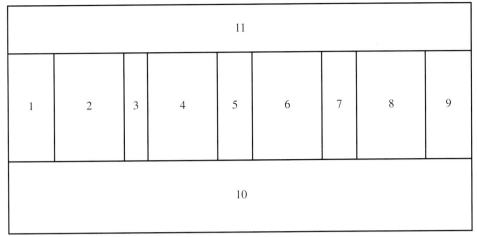

Schoolhouse top floor
(windows)

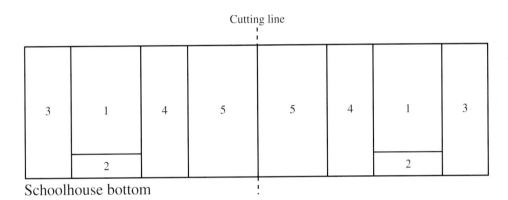

Schoolhouse bottom
floor (doors)

School walk

Kid blocks

PUMPKIN PATCH

12" x 13", by the author.

Oh, the possibilities of a pumpkin!

Quilt size: 12" x 13"

Fabric

Brown: Fat quarter
Yellow: Fat eighth
Orange: At least 2" x 15"
Autumnal mix: Varied scraps in autumn colors

Prewash, starch, and press fabric before cutting.

Cutting

Orange:

5 squares, 1½" x 1½" (5 pumpkins)
2 rectangles, 1½" x 2" (2 fat pumpkins)

Autumnal mix:

1 strip, ½" x 10" (bottom inside border)
24 rough-cuts, 2¼" x 3½" (tree branches)

Brown:

4 strips, 2" x 14" (outside border)
2 pieces, 1" x 2½" (tree trunks)
Strip to equal 1¼" x 58" (binding)

Yellow:

2 pieces, 2½" x 2¼" (background)
1 piece, 2½" x 4" (background)
28 squares, ¾" x ¾" (pumpkin background)
3 strips, ¾" x 10" (inside border)

14" x 15" piece for backing
14" x 15" piece of batting

Construction

Referring to figure 1, cut the 24 tree-branch rough-cuts in half diagonally, as indicated. You will cut 12 rough-cuts from the top left to the bottom right, and the other 12 from the top right to the bottom left.

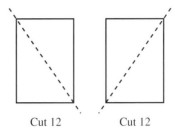

Cut 12   Cut 12

Fig. 1

See page 7 for instructions on freezer-paper piecing. Trace the number of tree branch patterns indicated on page 51 on the dull side of freezer paper. Lay the diagonally-cut tree branch pieces out on your TV tray and arrange them until you like the visual effect. Now is the time to change things out! When satisfied, piece the branches for the trees on the freezer-paper pattern.

Copy the tree trunks and background pattern (page 51) on freezer paper. Piece and sew yellow and brown fabrics. On the trunk, lift the freezer paper where needed to iron the trunk seam back to itself. Place the freezer paper back down, align along the seam, and iron down.

Draw a diagonal line on the back of each of the ¾" yellow squares. Place a small yellow square in the corner of each of the orange squares and rectangles, and sew along the diagonal line. Cut out the yellow corner close to the seam—don't cut the background of the pumpkin. See figure 2. Press the yellow squares to the corners. Sew a yellow square to each corner of each orange square and rectangle.

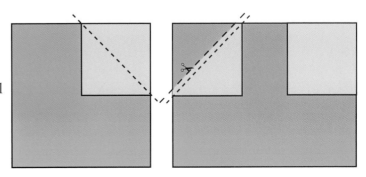

Fig. 2

Lay out the blocks following the quilt photo. Sew the branch strips together. Sew the yellow blocks with the trunks to the bottom of the branches. Sew the pumpkins together, then sew the pumpkin strip to the tree-trunk base. Block should measure 8½" wide by 9½" long at this point.

Sew in the pumpkin stems with embroidery floss, or free-motion stitch them with tearaway underneath.

> To help stabilize the pumpkin strip, cut two pieces of freezer paper 1" x 8". Iron one to the back of the pumpkins, leaving ¼" seam allowance all around. Iron the other piece to the bottom of the tree-trunk piece, leaving ¼" seam allowance. Pin baste and sew together along the edge of the freezer paper.

Borders

See page 14 for instructions on borders and refer to the quilt photo.

Inside border: Sew two of the 10" yellow strips to the sides, cut to fit. Sew a yellow 10" strip to the top, and use the autumnal mix 10" strip on the bottom, cutting to fit.

Outside border: Use brown 14" strips, cut to fit.

Finishing and Binding

See page 14 for tips on finishing. Square up the quilt. Layer the top over the batting and backing. Pin baste. Quilt as desired.

See page 11 for instructions on how to make and attach binding.

Make It Your Own!

▼ A simple quilt using just the tree-branch pattern in a variety of hand-dyes, or a range of one color would be very striking. Add more branch rows to make the trees whatever size you want.

▼ This could be a spring or summer quilt. Change the fall leaves to spring green and change the pumpkins to grass (use the August grass strip), and/or flowers (use the April Flower blocks).

Quilts In My Cubicle
Barbara Holtzman
Holyoke, Colorado
"Pumpkin Patch"
12" x 13"
October 2007

PUMPKIN PATCH tree trunks and background pattern

Enlarge above pattern 125%

Make 2

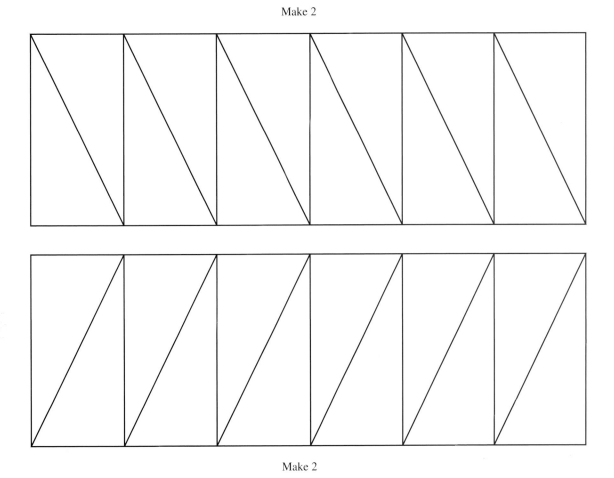

Make 2

PUMPKIN PATCH TREE BRANCH patterns

TURKEY TRACKS

12" x 12", by the author.

Run, turkey, run!

Quilt size: 12" square

Fabric

Blue paisley: Fat quarter
Orange-brown: Fat eighth
Brown: At least 5" x 7"
Orange: Fat eighth
Blue "sky": Fat eighth

> This quilt is helped tremendously by the type of fabric you pick. Look for variety and interest in the prints.

Prewash, starch, and press fabric before cutting.

Cutting

Blue paisley:
7 rough-cut strips, ¾" × 6" (side feathers)
4 strips 2" × 14" (outside border)
Strips to equal 1¼" × 56" (binding)

Orange-brown:
7 rough-cut strips, 2" × 8" (main feathers)
4 strips ¾" × 12" (first inside border)

Brown:
2 rough-cut strips, 2" × 6" (feather tops)

Orange:
4 strips, ¾" × 12" (second inside border)
Scraps to piece head

14" square for backing
14" square of batting

Construction

See page 7 for instructions on paper piecing. Copy the turkey pattern on page 55. Cut the pattern into strips A – G. Lay out the turkey pieces following the numerical order of the pattern pieces, checking and changing out your colors as desired. Sew the feather strips in sequence. Sew the turkey-head unit onto its feather strip before the strips are joined. Press. Trim just the sides of each feather strip.

Lay the strips in order following the turkey pattern and quilt photo. Pin baste to align seams, and sew the strips together. Add the corner pieces H and I. Press well and trim the block to 8½" × 8½".

Borders

See page 14 for instructions on borders.

First inside border: Use the brown 12" strips, cut to fit. The strips should measure 8½" each side and 9" top and bottom.

Second inside border: Use the orange 12" strips, cut to fit. The strips should measure 9" each side and 9½" top and bottom.

Outside border: Use blue paisley 14" strips, cut to fit. See page 10 for instructions on mitered corners.

Finishing and Binding

Pull out the pattern paper from the quilt. See page 14 for tips on finishing. Square up the quilt. Layer the top over the batting and backing. Pin baste. Quilt as desired.

See page 11 for instructions on how to make and attach binding.

▼ Without the turkey head, you have a type of fan. Make four blocks in a circular or wave pattern. See figure 1.

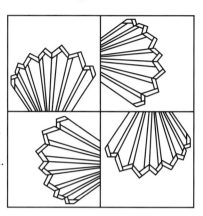

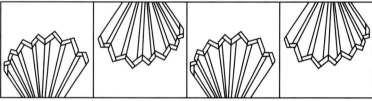

Fig. 1

Make It Your Own!

▼ For an exciting larger quilt, alternate blocks of "feathers" with Fireworks blocks (July quilt, CELEBRATE, page 37).

▼ Play with shapes and colors by alternating "feather" and "fireworks" strips in one Fan block.

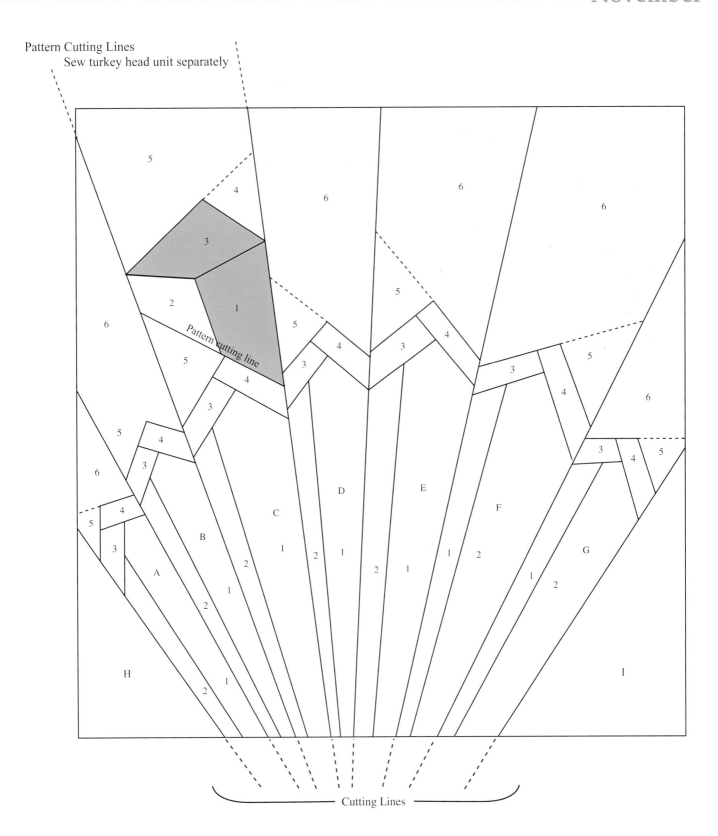

Pattern Cutting Lines
Sew turkey head unit separately

Pattern cutting line

Cutting Lines

TURKEY TRACKS pattern

Enlarge pattern 125%

STARRY NIGHT

12½" × 12½", by the author.

Wish upon a star!

Quilt Size: 12½" square
Block size: 4" square

Fabric

Red: Fat quarter
Green: At least 10" × 12"
Gold: At least 10" × 15"

Prewash, starch, and press fabric before cutting.

Cutting

Red:
Rough-cuts strip, 3" × 15"
1 square, 3½" × 3½"
4 strips, 2" × 13" (outside border)
Strips to equal 1¼" × 58" (binding)

Green:
Rough-cut strip, 3" × 15"
4 strips, 1" × 9" (inside border)

Gold:
2 rough-cut strips, 3" × 15"
3 squares, 3½" × 3½"

14" square for backing
14" square of batting

Construction

The following triangles and quarter-triangles don't need to be cut exactly; these are rough-cuts only.

For quarter-square triangles: Cut the 3½" squares (1 red, 3 gold) diagonally from corner to corner.

For triangles: Trace the template pattern on page 58 onto a small sheet of plastic and cut it out. Use the plastic template as a guide to cut triangles from your rough-cut strips.

See page 7 for instructions on freezer-paper piecing—they will be especially helpful in this instance, as the pattern for this quilt is used as an example!

Copy each freezer-paper pattern twice. Using each pattern two times, piece 8 half-blocks in number order with the rough-cut triangles. Check the sewing on the final triangle of each half to make sure it comes to a nice point before adding the corner quarter-triangles.

Use the quilt photo as a guide to pair off and lay out the half-blocks. Make sure there will be 3 gold corners and 1 red corner to each block—placement is important! Sew the halves together into blocks. Press the seam allowances open and trim each block to 4½". Lay out the 4 blocks as shown in the quilt photo, placing the 4 red quarter-triangles together at the center. Pin baste the upper blocks to the lower blocks, carefully aligning seams. Sew and press well. Pin baste the vertical center seam, carefully aligning seams. Sew and press.

Borders

See page 14 for instructions on borders and refer to the quilt photo.

Inside border: Use the green 9" strips, cut to fit. They should measure 8½" each side and 9" top and bottom. Press to the outside edge.

Outside border: Use the red 13" strips, cut to fit. Press to the outside edge.

December

Finishing and Binding

Remove the freezer paper. See page 14 for tips on finishing. Square up the quilt. Layer the top over the batting and backing. Pin baste. Quilt as desired.

See page 11 for instructions on how to make and attach binding.

Make It Your Own!

▼ This block would also work for the March block, since it looks like the blades of a windmill. Use "windy" material, blue sky, and rusty blades.

▼ The Kaleidoscope block is a fun one to work with in a large quilt. Your eye can make circles out of straight lines! Check the Internet for design ideas. Light and dark contrast is very important with this block.

▼ Adding "glitz" makes this a very Christmasy quilt. Try gold metallic thread or even gold fabric paint to add dots or short lines in a swirly pattern.

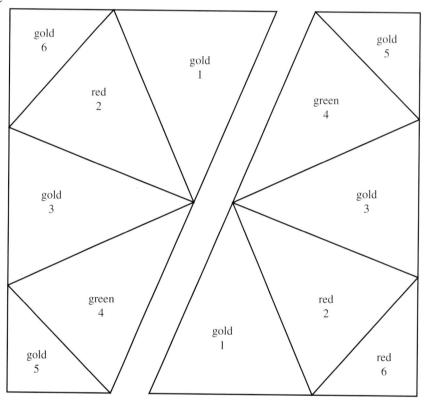

STARRY NIGHT freezer-paper patterns.
Copy each twice.

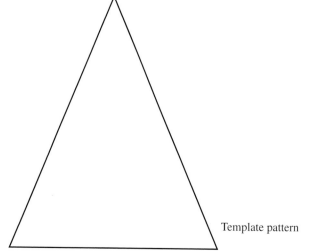

Template pattern

Hanging the Quilt

You've spent the time to decide on fabric and have carefully cut and sewn it together, from each little block to the binding. Now you're ready to display it!

There are several ways to display your quilt for life in a cubicle. One way is to simply pin it into the cubicle's fabric wall. Use small-headed or glass pins and they'll practically disappear. Or you can choose color-coordinated pins or find some antique hat pins.

I like to sew a rod pocket on my quilts in case I have a real wall I want to hang them on, and it can also be used to hang your quilt in your cubicle. There are Web sites where you can buy simple or decorative wire hangers.

Office supply stores such as Office Depot sell coat hooks made to fit over cubicle walls. Use one to hang a wire hanger or two to hold a dowel slid through a quilt sleeve. You can also find Fellowes® Partitions Additions™ Spring Clips at office supply stores. The clips have pins on the back that slide into a cubicle fabric wall. Open the clip to grip the edge of a quilt with no damage to it whatsoever. You'll need two or three clips to carry the weight of a quilt.

Another hanging option is to use Velcro® brand hook and loop tape. Cut a loop piece the length of your rod pocket or the width of your quilt. Sew along the rod pocket. Pin an equal length of the hook piece to your cubicle wall. Mount the quilt.

Be as creative displaying your quilt as you were in making it!

Hanging Resources

Country Quilts & Fabrics
218 E. 3rd Street
Kimball, Nebraska 69145
308-235-2717
www.countryquiltsnfabric.com

Patchwork & Paint
1031 N. 500 W.
Orem, Utah 84057
801-376-8152
www.patchworkandpaint.com

Robinson's Wood Crafts
www.robinsonswoodcrafts.com

For cubicle wall hooks and clips:

Office Depot
www.officedepot.com

Hanging the Quilt

Hanging rods can be made of almost anything, like this one, which was a curtain rod in a former life. Wooden dowels are inexpensive and can be painted to match the quilt or your cubicle.

Splurge on a nifty wire hanger that echoes the theme of your quilt. This star hanger would also work with SNOWBALL FIGHT or STARRY NIGHT.

Even a low-tech hanging plan can be color-coordinated. See how the yellow pin brings out the Schoolhouse block's yellow windows? A whole row of colored pins would mirror the kids' clothing.

If your quilt doesn't have a rod pocket, improvise! Ordinary clothespins come to the rescue here. When not holding a quilt, this cute hanger holds a shawl for chilly days.

Quilt Labels

I've read that "It's not a quilt until it's quilted," but for *me*, it's not a quilt until it's quilted – and the *label* is on!

There have been times when I've been finishing a quilt that the label is the last thing on my mind. But other times I plan all along the making of the quilt how I want to make the label "coordinate" with the quilt top. On certain patterns I mention to make extra blocks, so when it comes time to put the quilt together, you have other choices for arranging the blocks. Those extra blocks come in handy when you're ready to do the label. Then again, sometimes blocks don't turn out as nice as we'd like them to. Add them to the top, sides, or wherever they seem to work best to add to your signature block.

Be creative and analyze your quilt. Is there an element you can simplify to make a block for your label? Are there some scrap pieces that can be recut to make an edge for your label? Simplify and use your imagination. Make it *your own*!

I stabilize the signature block with freezer paper to write the important information, such as name, date, title, and address with a fine tip permanent pen. To make the label itself easier to sew down, I take extra binding, cut it down to ¾" wide, and sew it around the sides and top like the binding on the quilt top, turning the corners as in the directions for sewing on binding. It makes a clean edge for your important information. Sew it on by hand along the lower edge of the quilt back before you sew on your binding.

Remember – there are no *bad* blocks, only blocks that can be creatively changed into a label!

My mother taught me to sew in junior high and I used that skill to make clothes for a long time—through high school and college. My first quilting project was a hand-pieced bed quilt that took me over five years to complete.

Then small quilts caught my attention, especially miniature quilts. Because I *do* have a full-time job but enjoy sewing, the idea of making a small quilt appealed to me. I could actually finish that! Plus it's fun to display the quilts on a wall and admire them (and have them admired!)

As I made more quilts, my attention was drawn to the competition side of quilting. Trying to make a quilt good enough to enter into competition helped me get better at piecing, quilting, and all aspects of making a quilt. The design element drew me in because it was another way to be creative. While I enjoy my job, I also need something to do that is creative and different. Quilting fills this need. I can pick a simple, easy quilt or a complicated design. It's the whole process I enjoy—from picking out the fabric to putting on that last stitch in the binding.

Writing this book gave me a chance to explore an idea that I've had for a long time— quilts in my (work) cubicle! I liked the idea of a quilt a month. I realize time is limited for many women—our lives are so busy—but managing to take time here and there to create something results in a great deal of satisfaction.

Barbara Holtzman

For todays quilters...
inspiration and creativity from
AQS Publishing

7601
us $26.95

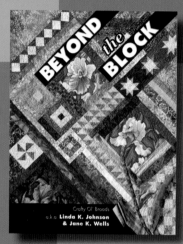

7611
us $26.95

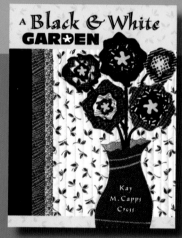

7605
us $24.95

7769
us $26.95

7609
us $19.95

7772
us $26.95